FAITH

OVER

FEAR

BREAKING FREE FROM
THE GRIP OF FEAR

GARY KEESEE

Published by Free Indeed Publishing.
Distributed by Faith Life Now.

Faith Life Now
P.O. Box 779
New Albany, OH 43054
1-(888)-391-LIFE

You can reach Faith Life Now on the Internet at www.faithlifenow.com.

CONTENTS

THE CALL TO CONQUER FEAR

If you're holding this book in your hands, it's not by accident. I believe God led you to this book because He has something incredible in store for you—something bigger than you've ever imagined. But let me tell you right from the start, the journey to discovering what God has for you isn't about simply sitting back and waiting for things to happen. It's about taking action—decisive, faith-filled action—that breaks the chains of fear and propels you into the life you were meant to live.

I know what it's like to be gripped by fear. I've been there. Fear has a way of creeping into every corner of your life and whispering lies that hold you back from pursuing your dreams, stepping out in faith, and living the abundant life God has promised. But here's the truth—fear is a lie. It's an enemy that must be confronted, exposed, and defeated. And the good news is, you don't have to do it alone. God has given you everything you need to overcome fear and walk boldly in His promises.

Throughout this book, we're going to tackle fear head-on. We'll uncover the root of fear, explore the truths of God's Word, and learn practical, powerful strategies to live life free from the paralyzing effects of fear. You'll discover how to change the picture in your mind, align your heart with God's promises, and fully step into the authority and destiny He has for you.

But let me warn you—this isn't a book for the passive. It's not for those who are content with living in the shadow of fear. This is for the courageous, the bold, and those who are ready to rise up and take hold of the life God has promised. If you're ready to break free, if you're ready to live with the kind of faith that moves mountains, then you're in the right place.

So, let's begin this journey together. It's time to put faith over fear once and for all. As you read, my prayer is that you'll be inspired, challenged, and equipped to live a life that's free from fear and is full of God's power, purpose, and peace.

Let's get started.

—Gary Keesee

CHAPTER ONE

IS FEAR HOLDING YOU HOSTAGE?

I was raised with fear. I bet you were too. Fear permeates our culture.

But you were not born with fear—you learned it. We all did. We grew up in the valley of the shadow of death. We were trained in fear by a perverted culture. We all grew up thinking about how to build walls around our lives to protect us against the inevitable onslaught of problems.

But fear is a lie.

You may not have realized that fear is an enemy in your life. It is your absolute enemy and should be cast aside immediately. You must learn how to handle fear, or fear will handle you.

Fear is not part of the Kingdom of God, and so it is not part of your future. You can decide right now that you are going to take the Word of God at face value—and then you do not have to be afraid anymore.

> *Yea, though I walk through the valley of the shadow of death, I will fear no evil: for thou art with me; thy rod and thy staff they comfort me.*
> —Psalm 23:4 (KJV)

Picture a shepherd walking along with a rod and a staff. The staff is to lead the sheep, and the rod is to keep little feet moving in the right direction—and away from the cliff.

Jesus is our Good Shepherd (John 10:14). You can trust Jesus to get you where you need to go. His rod and His staff will lead you and protect you in life. And why do you not need to fear evil? Because God is with you.

You must learn to trust Jesus because we live in the shadow of death. In other words, everything around us smells of death, sounds of death, and looks like death. Sickness is a slow form of death. Poverty is a slow form of death. The media talks constantly of death.

You have to practice trusting Jesus. You have to know who He is and know who you are because you will not win in life just by going to church on Sunday mornings for one hour a week.

Problems demand an answer, and it is nice to know you have the answer.

Years ago, when my wife, Drenda, and I were students at Oral Roberts University in Tulsa, Oklahoma, we went to Kansas to hunt with some friends. We hunted all day, and then that night, on our way home in our old, beat-up Toyota Corolla with something like 300,000 miles on it, the car broke down.

We stepped out of the car and looked around. There was nothing around us. But far off in the distance, we thought we saw one of those mercury lights on some guy's barn. We started walking in that direction.

When we got there, the farmer was so generous. He immediately invited us in.

It was Sunday night, and we were about a seven-hour drive from Tulsa. As it happened, Drenda had just been hired for a brand-new position, and her new job started on Monday morning. The farmer thought for a minute, then said, "I will drive you home."

He hitched up a trailer, put the old Toyota on top of the trailer, and then drove us all night.

We got to Tulsa an hour or two before Drenda had to

go to work. The man would not take any money for gas. He was a believer, as you may have guessed, and I still remember how good it felt to have someone there to rescue us and to take care of the problem.

When God is with you, the bottom line is that He always has an answer for you. You have no reason to fear. Whatever it is, He will take care of it. He is going to make a way.

> *Who hath delivered us from the power of darkness, and hath translated us into the kingdom of his dear Son.*
>
> —Colossians 1:13 (KJV)

We do not want to make concessions to darkness. We do not want to make an agreement with darkness because we have been set in place in the Kingdom—the Kingdom of Light—and we have been given the authority of the Kingdom.

If you are walking in darkness and you have a flashlight, you can just turn on the flashlight, and then you are not in the dark anymore. The light always wins.

But then fear says, "What happens if the flashlight stops working or the batteries go dead?" You buy a second flashlight and more batteries.

If you continue to follow fear's promptings, you will never get to the end of preparing for the worst. So often, we try to free our lives from fear, build more walls, and prepare for everything so our fears cannot find us or trap us.

You keep buying flashlights, and you keep buying more batteries, and you keep preparing for the problem—but fear is always going to give you another problem.

And it will never end.

You simply cannot make concessions to fear because fear is only going to hold you hostage.

> *Fear thou not; for I am with thee: be not dismayed; for I am thy God: I will strengthen thee; yea, I will help thee; yea, I will uphold thee with the right hand of my righteousness.*
>
> —Isaiah 41:10 (KJV)

Why should you not be afraid? Because God is with you. You are not alone.

This is why so many of us enjoy Marvel's Avengers movies. We love our heroes! Because heroes are not afraid—they are *never* afraid. We cheer them on because they just jump right into the problem and they deal with it.

We need to see ourselves as "God's Avengers." We are to boldly jump right into problems and bring righteousness to bear in the situation. We are to set the captives free. We are to represent the Kingdom of God.

This means you are the answer. You are someone's hero. And you need to get that thought into your mind because heroes think differently than victims. You are not a victim, so you need to stop thinking that way. You are a hero.

You are God's Avenger. You have been anointed by the King who made everything you can see. You are His child. He loves you. There is nothing held against you. Your sin is removed as far as the east is from the west. You have been made righteous through Jesus Christ. It is time for you to stop practicing failure and stop thinking about fear.

When I was growing up, my parents had a housekeeper. Every day before she came to work, she would find the worst story in *The Columbus Dispatch,* clip it out, and bring it with her to the house—which seems crazy to me now that I am old enough to understand spiritual truth.

But every day, she would lay the article on the kitchen table. "Did you hear about this?" she would ask, and then she would tell us about the most horrible thing that had happened the previous night. This went on for years! I did not think about how it affected me at the time, but it did affect me!

What are you feeding on? You have a choice—and you are going to become what you feed on.

I grew up trying to avoid stress. I was raised with that attitude. I sat in the back of the class. I never volunteered to be in a place that was scary or a place that could make me feel insecure. I held back because it just felt safer that way. Have you ever felt that way?

When I was born again, God called me to preach and sent me to college. Now, for me, that sounded absolutely nuts.

Growing up, I ran my dad's pizza shops in New Albany, Ohio. Since I had grown up there, you might think I would know some things about the area. But I stayed in this little circle and never went very far. I remember when I was a senior in high school, we went down to the Ohio River and crossed the bridge into Kentucky. And I remember thinking, *Wow, I'm in another state!*

You may know that I love the outdoors and love to hunt. I hunted growing up. I ran a trap line. I subscribed to magazines like *Field & Stream* and read them cover to cover, poring over the catalogs that sold hunting and fishing gear. But I never thought about going to any of the places I read about—that would have been too scary! It was too far outside of my comfort zone. I was so trained not to expand my vision that it never even occurred to me to venture out. In fact, I never saw the mountains of Colorado until I was 40. And if you think I was a sad case, I agree with you.

I still remember driving to Tulsa when God called me to school. It was scary. It was far away. Later, when God called me into insurance sales, it was even worse because I was so afraid of talking to people.

But God had to train me. He had to push me past my comfort zone because my destiny was not where I lived. It was out in front of me. And I had to get there. Fear is going to hold you hostage if you let it. You have to overcome it.

I went into sales, and I was afraid of people. And because I was living on commissions and at the time did not know how the Kingdom operated, I was always under a lot of stress. But I kept pushing myself and pushing myself; and one morning, I woke up basically paralyzed—my arms numb, legs numb, and face numb. My body had just shut down. The doctors could not determine what was wrong with me.

I was paralyzed. I had money problems. I was a mess.

But I got a message.

My problem was not the paralysis. My problem was not the lack of money. The problems I was trying to deal with were not the real problems.

Darkness is not the problem. It is the fear of darkness that is the problem.

Then he got into the boat and his disciples followed him. Suddenly a furious storm came up on the lake, so that the waves swept over the boat. But Jesus was sleeping. The disciples went and woke him, saying, "Lord, save us! We're going to drown!"

He replied, "You of little faith, why are you so afraid?" Then he got up and rebuked the winds and the waves, and it was completely calm.

—Matthew 8:23–26 (NIV)

There was this big storm, but what was Jesus doing? He was sleeping. The issue for Jesus was not the storm. He was sleeping. The issue was the disciples' lack of faith.

In the same way, the root of your fear is not your bills or your sickness or whatever it is you are facing right now. Your problem is not your problem.

The darkness is not your problem. It is the fear of the darkness. It is the fear of the sickness. It is the fear of money problems. It is the fear that is holding you hostage. The problem is the fear you have trained yourself to believe.

Jesus has given you the keys to the Kingdom. You have light and you have answers, but it is the fear you have taught yourself to believe about the problem that becomes the problem.

"If I can just get through this storm..."
"If I can just pay off this debt..."
"If I can just get well again..."
"If I can just solve this problem..."
"If I can just overcome this obstacle..."

But you have not recognized what the real problem is here. These are simply the symptoms of the problem. You are trying to avoid fearful situations.

We have to go to the root. Fear is a deception, and it will try to make an agreement with you.

We knew a lady who was around 80 or so, and she lived alone. Her front door had about six dead bolts on it. When you entered her house, the door to the next room also had multiple dead bolts on it. Down the hallway was her bedroom, and her bedroom door had multiple dead bolts on it. Someone should have told her that there are not enough dead bolts in the world to stop fear. She lived her life as a prisoner in her own house. And that is what fear is going to do.

The disciples shook Jesus awake. "Help! We are going to drown!"

These were professional fishermen who knew about storms. They really thought they were going to drown. But Jesus was sleeping.

But there is something they should have remembered about this boat ride. Just before they departed, Jesus had told the disciples they were going over to the other side of the lake (Matthew 8:18). And when Jesus says you are going over to the other side of the lake, there are not enough demons in hell or big enough storms to stop you from getting there.

And if Jesus says that by His stripes you are healed, there are no demons in hell that can stop you from receiving that healing—or whatever it is you need.

But you can stop it. Your fear can stop it.

You need to stop saying what fear is saying and start saying what God says about your situation.

The seventy-two returned with joy and said, "Lord, even the demons submit to us in your name."

[Jesus] replied, "I saw Satan fall like lightning from heaven. I have given you authority to trample on snakes and scorpions and to overcome all the power of the enemy; nothing will harm you."

—Luke 10:17–19 (NIV)

What is your definition of the word "nothing"? The King James translation of the Bible says it this way: *"Nothing shall by any means hurt you"* (Luke 10:19b, KJV).

Friend, if you have that kind of authority and that kind of protection, what do you possibly have to fear? Fear is absent in the Kingdom. It is not part of Kingdom life, and it is not part of your life.

You have the authority to trample on snakes and scorpions. That means you are going forward. You will get across the lake. Fear tries to hinder you from going anywhere. Fear tells you to stop or even back up. But you trample on snakes and scorpions. You are moving right along, and Satan has no authority to slow you down.

When I experienced that paralysis, I went to the doctors for tests, and they gave me all kinds of futuristic prophecies: "Your body is all whacked out," they told me. "You have got to cut this and that out of your diet. You have got to restrict that. You have got to change how you live, confine yourself to this, and limit yourself to that."

I found myself agreeing with what they said. *"Well, I guess I could live without that."*

I decided I would rather limit myself than die. I got to the place where I was afraid to leave my house. I became a prisoner in my own body.

Fear is hell on earth. The Bible says with fear, there is torment (1 John 4:18). But we have been delivered from fear.

One day, as I was going through all this, Drenda wisely said, "Stop. You cannot do this." She saw that I had begun to make concessions.

She asked me, "Do you want to live this way?"

I said, "No."

"Fine," she said. So, she took the medicine, threw it in the toilet, and flushed it down.

Thank God for a godly wife. I had to learn that we never win when we make concessions to fear.

On another occasion, I went to the dentist; and when he injected me with Novocaine, like a flash, my face instantly became numb.

"Hey," I told him, "My whole face is numb."

"I must have hit the nerve," he said, "Well, about 80% of the time, that will just heal up by itself."

Later, I was at a friend's house and foolishly told him what had happened. My friend said, "Oh my God! My uncle's face is completely paralyzed! The dentist hit his nerve. He's paralyzed for life."

Since I had never in my life heard of anyone being paralyzed by the dentist, I foolishly asked someone else. The second person said the same thing, "Oh, my aunt is completely paralyzed!"

I learned to stop asking questions.

The reason we need to stop asking those kinds of questions is because those people do not have any authority. We need to ask Jesus and find out what He has to say about it.

So that night, I could not sleep. Insomnia. Fear can keep you awake at night. As I was lying there, I remembered that my dad had Bell's palsy a couple of years earlier.

As I understand it, there is a nerve that controls the muscles in your face. It is right below your ear, and when the area gets inflamed, it pinches the nerve. Then, that whole side of the face stops working. My dad could not close his mouth. He could not close his eyes. His entire face drooped. And that night, a little voice said to me, "You have a little twinge, right? That could be Bell's palsy!" And sure enough, I did feel a little twinge.

I woke up the next morning with full-blown Bell's palsy. I could not close my mouth; I could not close my eyes. I went to the doctor, and he checked me out. "Yes, Sir," he said. "You have a full-blown case of Bell's palsy."

Then he said, "Well, about 80% of the time, it heals up. Only about 20% have permanent paralysis."

I knew better than to ask anyone else. And I was not going to ask another doctor.

Because I knew my problem was not my problem.

My problem was that I did not have faith. My problem was that I needed to find out what Jesus had to say about it. I decided to go no further down the road of fear. I would make no more concessions to it. To help me focus on the Word of God, Drenda posted notes with Scriptures all over the house.

One of these Scriptures was:

> *Surely he took up our pain and bore our suffering, yet we considered him punished by God, stricken by him, and afflicted. But he was pierced for our transgressions, he was crushed for our iniquities; the punishment that brought us peace was on him, and by his wounds we are healed.*
> —Isaiah 53:4–5 (NIV)

And so, for about three or four days, I read these Scriptures as I walked through the house, and then one day, walking down the hall, I glanced at this Scripture card again, and suddenly—*Bam!* The anointing of God hit me, and I instantly knew I was free. The fear stopped talking to me, and my face returned to normal within an hour. I was completely healed!

We have to learn how to handle fear. Fear will try to tell you to make concessions and take a step back. It will tell you that you are not, that you cannot, and that you will not. Fear will try to bounce you into a corner, and you cannot let it do that! You have to stop it short, because it is all a lie.

The Bible says, *"For the Spirit God gave us does not make us timid, but gives us power, love and self-discipline"* (2 Timothy 1:7, NIV).

Another version says, *"For God has not given us a spirit of fear, but of power and of love and of a sound mind"* (2 Timothy 1:7, NKJV).

As we consider how to get free from fear, how to overcome fear, and how to deal with fear, we need to lay the groundwork. The enemy is lying to you through fear. He is trying to push you into a corner, but you are bigger than you think you are.

Your potential is greater than you think it is. You can do greater things than you think because God is in you. And the enemy knows that if you ever find out who you really are and understand the authority you have been given, you can do some real damage. He knows that when you share your story, your experience will also set others free.

Fear is going to keep trying to get you to back up, to get you to make concessions, and to get you to go out and buy some more dead bolts. Fear will try to tell you that you are incapable, that you are not lovely, that you are an idiot. Fear will start naming adjectives about your life that do not match up with what Jesus says about you. I am here today to say that it is up to you to change the picture.

CHAPTER TWO

CHANGE THE PICTURE.

Most Americans get exposed to a heavy dose of fear every day because almost all of the media around us is built on fear. And if you continually feed on tragedy, loss, and fear, you will keep getting results you do not like—because you are programming yourself to believe in fear.

Statistics show that prescriptions for drugs to mitigate fear have reached record heights. This is why I say that if you do not deal with fear, fear will deal with you. I lived through that for nine years—panic attacks, antidepressants, and all kinds of dysfunction. I got the T-shirt, but believe me. This is not something you want to experience.

> *Yea, though I walk through the valley of the shadow of death, I will fear no evil: for thou art with me; thy rod and thy staff they comfort me.*
> —Psalm 23:4 (KJV)

When we are in the valley of the shadow of death, however, Psalm 23 says we are to fear no evil. If we look up the word "no" in a dictionary, we see it means "none." Because God is with us, there is no need to fear.

The Hebrew phrase for "shadow of death" literally

means "darkness," but not just darkness. It means "deep darkness." It suggests distress, extreme danger, and a place of the dead.

We all grew up in that valley of the shadow of fear and death surrounded by the stench of things dying, bad things happening to people all around us, perverted things on TV and in the media, and all the disappointments of life.

Which is why we immediately begin to put up walls and protections. "If I can just get enough money, I will be okay." We begin to design our lives to avoid fear; and before long, we have backed ourselves into a corner. Then, quite literally, we are being held hostage by our fear.

> *The people living in darkness have seen a great light;*
> *on those living in the land of the shadow of death a*
> *light has dawned.*
> —Matthew 4:16 (NIV)

If you were in complete, absolute, deep darkness, what would you do? Sit down? If you did, nothing more would happen in your life. You would stop moving forward. You would just sit.

Did you know that most people live in that kind of survival state? They have given up their dreams because their fear is too great to even try. They are afraid to hope because they do not want to be disappointed. So, they just sit in darkness.

But human beings are not designed to sit still. We are designed to enjoy life. As far as life goes, God's people should be the most filled with life and as full of vision as anybody on Earth.

This is why it is so important for us to understand how fear works. When people sitting in darkness see a great light, they can see—because light is there. Their vision returns. When you turn on a flashlight in the dark, the light always wins over the darkness.

You are not of the kingdom of darkness. You are of the Kingdom of Light.

God always wins. You always win. You have to constantly think this way because if you program yourself for failure, you will fail—perhaps without even realizing that you are sitting in darkness.

Last night when you turned on the lights in your home, did you pray before you flipped the light switch on? Had you been interceding and fasting during the day so that the lights would come on in the evening?

Well, why not?

Because you had absolute confidence that the lights would come on.

But that would not have been true back long ago. A thousand years ago, if someone in your neighborhood had seen your lights, they would have been completely shocked. Yet you barely give it any thought at all. Why is that?

Because you have renewed your mind to the concept of lights and the law of electricity, you understand that this law never changes. It works here. It works in Africa. It works on the North Pole. Wherever there is electricity, you can have light. You enjoy lights every day, and you do not even think about it—because you understand the laws at work.

In the same way that you understand the laws of electricity and how they work, you also need to understand that the Kingdom of God is a kingdom of laws.

I was sitting next to a guy on a plane last year, and he was literally digging his fingers into the seat. He was sweating. He was nervous. I think he was actually shaking. I was concerned about him, so I asked him what the problem was. He said, "This is the first time that I have ever been on a plane." Fear had overtaken him. Why? Because he had experienced more gravity than planes in his life.

This guy knew that at 30,000 feet, in his world, gravity says, "You are going down."

But I fly on planes all the time, and I am also a pilot, so I have experienced the law of lift multiple times. My mind is renewed to how the law of lift operates. So, I am no longer shocked when the plane takes off. I anticipate and am totally confident that the plane will hold me at 30,000 feet. But this was this guy's first time, and all he knew was the law of gravity. He had not experienced the law of lift, so he reacted from his experience and anticipated what the law he understood would produce. And for him, it produced the fear that the plane would fall.

Now, notice that Paul reminds us in Romans, "*Through Christ Jesus the law of the Spirit who gives life has set you free from the law of sin and death*" (Romans 8:2, NIV). Notice there are two kingdoms here and that both kingdoms have laws.

There is the law of the Spirit of life through Christ and the law of sin and death, the shadow of death, and fear. If you want to be free from fear, you must change your understanding of the laws, just like that guy on the plane who only knew the law of gravity. He had not studied. He had not flown. He had not renewed his mind to the law of lift. So, he was nervous and afraid. But I knew it was a law and would work every time. I was confident because I had renewed my mind to it.

It is the same with the law of the Spirit of life. Since it is a law, it implies that it has a function and process and that you can learn it. This is the law that God taught me when Drenda and I were in serious financial dysfunction and I was on antidepressants and had given up hope. He began to teach me about His Kingdom and the laws of His Kingdom.

As I began to meditate on His laws, I began to grow

more confident in those laws, and my fear subsided. In other words, I could sit back in that plane and enjoy the view. I was not nervous about it falling out of the sky. Life was no longer a journey of terror; it was a journey of opportunity. I began to see that this law that I was previously afraid of—this law of lift—could actually take me places that I could never have gone before. And so it is in the Kingdom of God.

As you learn more about the Kingdom of God, who you are in Christ, who God is, and how the laws of the Kingdom operate, a whole new world suddenly opens up to you.

You are no longer sitting in darkness trying to survive one more week. Your vision then sees that there is a whole life out there—the good life. God designed you to enjoy the good life, to have potential, to have your mind renewed to the laws of the Kingdom.

So, now you have a choice to make. You need to understand how the Kingdom operates and how these laws operate, because they never change. They work the same for everyone. A lot of Christians believe that if someone just prays hard enough and long enough, then

God might do something. But that is not true. He did something 2,000 years ago. He has *already* given you the Kingdom.

Friend, Jesus said that it was God's good pleasure to give it to you (Luke 12:32). God's Kingdom is not something that can be observed, because it is in you (Luke 17:20–21). You are a citizen of the Kingdom (Ephesians 2:19). You have legal rights to everything the Kingdom has in it. In fact, the Bible says you are "*heirs of God and co-heirs with Christ*" (Romans 8:17, NIV). Everything that Jesus owns, you own. Everything!

I trust that hope is rising up even now as you read these words and the picture of life in your spirit is changing. Why would your head be down? Why would you be discouraged? God is with you! Whom shall you fear? If God says you can do something, you can do it—because it is impossible for God to lie!

Paul reminds us in Colossians that "*[God] has rescued us from the dominion of darkness and brought us into the kingdom of the Son he loves*" (Colossians 1:13, NIV). Some translations say He brought us into the Kingdom of Light. You have changed kingdoms. You have changed governments. You have changed functions. But until you learn how the law of the Spirit of life operates, the only law you are accustomed to is the law of sin and death. And since sin and death are fear, you are going to be held hostage by that fear. You are going to be sitting in darkness, and you are going to have a life of hiding, which is no life at all.

So, you have to decide to learn the laws of the Kingdom. And let me just say this very plainly: *Stop all the begging!* God's Kingdom does not operate that way. If you are begging God for something, it means you have no clue how His Kingdom works. Because the Kingdom is always "Yes!" The Bible says every single promise is "Yes!"—not maybe, not if you lived a perfect life yesterday. They are always "Yes!" because you own the Kingdom. It is yours.

I do not know how you do things in your home, but my kids do not have to beg for breakfast. In fact, they expect it. When they were growing up, they never had to beg for breakfast. We did not require them to fast and pray for 21 days to get breakfast. Often, they acted like they owned it. Most of the time, they did not even say "Thank you." They just said, "Give me the cereal" or "Pass the milk" because they *did* own it. That is how it is in the Kingdom. You own it. "Give us this day our daily bread." Everything in the Kingdom is yours.

CHAPTER THREE

FAITH BEGINS WITH HOPE.

Shortly before dawn Jesus went out to them, walking on the lake. When the disciples saw him walking on the lake, they were terrified. "It's a ghost," they said, and cried out in fear.

But Jesus immediately said to them: "Take courage! It is I. Don't be afraid."

"Lord, if it's you," Peter replied, "tell me to come to you on the water."

"Come," he said.

Then Peter got down out of the boat, walked on the water and came toward Jesus. But when he saw the wind, he was afraid and, beginning to sink, cried out, "Lord, save me!"

Immediately Jesus reached out his hand and caught him. "You of little faith," he said, "why did you doubt?"

—Matthew 14:25–31 (NIV)

We have to give Peter credit because at least he understood some things about the Kingdom. First off, he knew, as a human being, that he could not walk on the water.

But still, he said, "*Lord, if it's you, tell me to come to you on the water.*"

Jesus said, "*Come.*"

Peter knew he could not do it by himself, but if Jesus said it, he knew he could. Peter did not walk on the water; he walked on the Word! But when he put his eyes back on his circumstances, his old training came into play. As a fisherman, he had seen storms on that lake many times. As he saw the wind and the waves, all of a sudden, his thinking reverted back to what he had known growing up his entire life. Before that moment, his experience was: "Wait a minute; this is not supposed to happen. You can drown out here. This is a storm. Wait a minute; I am in trouble." And when Peter's eyes went off the Word, he started to sink.

You and I have to face that same battle. Until you make a decision that you are going to look at the Word of God and not the circumstances, you are going to sink every time. You are going to fall into fear's trap. Satan will block you every time and say you have no authority, you have no power, and that you are doomed to have disease and die like everybody else. The enemy is going to paint the picture that you will just buy into.

As long as you feed on fear, you will live in fear. And unless you have the Word of God, you will not have a case to legally stand on. You will not be able to argue your case and say, "No, the Bible says: With long life you shall satisfy me" (Psalm 91:16). But when you make a decision to live according to what the book says and realize everything in the Word of God applies to you, then you are going to actually have it in your life and live the Kingdom lifestyle.

If you want to handle fear, you have to change the picture. You have been programmed with a picture of the shadow of death. Since you were born in the earthly realm, you have been under the fear that rules the earth. You have been programmed this way since you were little. But now, you have to challenge it. You are going to have to fight it. You must stand up against it, because it is lying to you.

The Bible says fear has torment (1 John 4:18), and I can tell you, after my nine years of fighting, being on antidepressants, and trying to find peace, it is literally hell on earth. And that is why I want to help you. I do not want you to go through it.

So, let me be as clear as possible about this. If you have fear today, it is because you have never been perfected in truth. The Bible says that if you know the truth, it will set you free (John 8:32).

The fact that you have fear is evidence to you that one, you are not in faith, and two, that you are not perfected in truth. In other words, fear is still your basis. The way you believe life should happen is still based on that old law of sin and death. It is up to you to renew your mind to the new law of life.

No one else can do it for you. It is between you and God. You need to remember who you are. You need to go out there and do what you need to do. This is your future. You must take the time and make the effort necessary to renew your mind. It is your choice. You have to decide as a person and a family to determine that "We are going to have what God says!"

"Do not conform to the pattern of this world, but be transformed by the renewing of your mind" (Romans 12:2, NIV).

In other words, do not think the thoughts of the world.

Do not be conformed to how the world thinks, that shadow of death, that law of sin and fear and death. Do not be conformed to that old way of thinking, but instead be transformed by the Word of God and begin to think the thoughts of God. Begin to say what God says about your situation. The Bible says that every promise of God is "Yes" and "Amen." So that means you already have it!

You need to change the picture. God's promises carry a picture. Fear also carries a picture.

Whenever you see or hear something fearful, it carries a picture. Either you reject that picture or you begin to meditate on it. The Bible says that the shield of faith—which means agreeing with what God says—rejects fear and quenches every fiery dart. The shield of faith automatically rejects fear as a nonessential possibility. It rejects it as a lie. It rejects it as nonsense. It cannot happen because you are fully persuaded by what God says.

But if you are not fully persuaded by what God says, then we are back again at the same issue. You have a truth problem. You are not perfected in truth. You are still in the place of being renewed to the spirit of sin and death. In reality, though, you have been given the Spirit of life, so you have to make a decision to be renewed to that truth. You have to change the picture.

Promises also carry a picture. If I said I would give you a chocolate chip cookie after church next Sunday, you would immediately know what a chocolate chip cookie looks like and whether or not you like chocolate chip cookies. But you would also anticipate the fact that a cookie after church would be too close to lunch. So, you might not accept a cookie, but you would thank me.

You could picture a chocolate chip cookie because you know what one looks like. You would understand what I was offering you because you know what a cookie is.

In the same way, as you renew your mind to what God says, you know what He is offering you. His promises carry a picture. When His promise says, *"By His stripes we are healed"* (Isaiah 53:5b, NKJV), you will see your healing with the same definition, the same confidence, and the same reality as you see that chocolate chip cookie—because you know what it looks like, smells like, and tastes like.

A promise of God changes the picture. Fear says you

are about to die from that hangnail. Fear amplifies the situation and says, "Oh no, it is too late for you! You are going down now!" But the Word of God tells you what God says about it. If you take hold of the promise of God, it carries a picture of your future. It changes the picture, and it alleviates fear.

You should also know that changing your picture to match God's promises gives hope, but it does not bring faith. A picture carries with it a possibility.

For example, if I promised you that chocolate chip cookie, in your mind's eye, you would see it, smell it, and would almost taste it. But someone still would have to bake the cookie.

So, there is another step involved in the process. Now, you have to accept that picture. A picture brings hope. Hope gives you a different picture of your future. Your next step is to engage in that future and walk it out.

> *And these signs will accompany those who believe:*
> *In my name they will drive out demons; they will*
> *speak in new tongues ... they will place their hands*
> *on sick people, and they will get well.*
> —Mark 16:17–18 (NIV)

These individual signs that accompany those who believe are not faith. These signs (this evidence, these miracles) point to your answer. When you see the picture (the evidence, the hope), your next question should be, "How did that happen? Because I might need that, I might want that, I may want to use that, so how did it happen?"

Several years ago, our daughter Amy had a tumor in her abdomen. Being a newlywed, she did not want a hysterectomy or surgery in that area because she wanted to have babies. She decided that as a citizen of God's Kingdom, she had a legal right to healing as the Word of God says, and so she chose to believe God for healing instead of undergoing surgery. And so that is what she did. First, she took about 30 days to review what the Word of God said about healing and became confident that healing was legally hers. Then we laid our hands on her and prayed for her.

Nothing happened at that moment. But two weeks later, she went to bed like normal and woke up the next morning thirteen pounds lighter and nine inches smaller in her waist. She did not feel anything during the night. She just woke up healed.

As it happened, Amy had an X-ray at a chiropractor's office about a week or so before she was healed. She has a copy of that X-ray that shows that big mass in her abdomen and her back straight and knotted. So, the week she was healed, she went back to the chiropractor and had a second X-ray. The mass was gone, and her spine was perfectly curved and perfectly remade by the power of God.

Perhaps as you read about Amy's healing, something began to change in what you picture. You may not have known that God still healed people. Maybe you thought miracles had all passed away. Your next thought may be, *How did that happen? I might need that one day.* Or you may be sick today, and your question is, "Is there a possibility that I could be healed?" And that answer would be "yes."

Of course, simply seeing a new picture is not enough to produce faith. Seeing it produces hope. Faith is always attached to the Word of God. But you have to begin with hope.

When I minister to someone with a problem, I always want to begin by showing them an answer—a new picture. This is so when they see the power of God in someone else's life, they are going to ask, "How could I have that?" And that is when you want to minister the Word of God to them. The evidence of the power of God brings the hope that opens the door for them to ask.

I trust you understand now why changing the picture is vital. When fear is talking to you, you have to get a new picture in your mind by meditating on what God says is your legal right.

Learning how the law of the Spirit of life operates and trusting God's laws to operate on your behalf is your key to freedom. As you become more comfortable with that law operating, fear loses its ground against your life. So, in that way, it is like boarding a plane. Flying is so common to me now that the thought of the plane crashing does not even cross my mind. It is foreign to me because my experience has been that the plane successfully flies every time. I know the law works. And so it is in the Kingdom of God.

CHAPTER FOUR

FULLY PERSUADED

When Jesus and His three closest disciples came down from what our Bible calls the "Mount of the Transfiguration," there was a crowd waiting for them at the bottom.

When they came to the crowd, a man approached Jesus and knelt before him. "Lord, have mercy on my son," he said. "He has seizures and is suffering greatly. He often falls into the fire or into the water. I brought him to your disciples, but they could not heal him."

"You unbelieving and perverse generation," Jesus replied, "how long shall I stay with you? How long shall I put up with you? Bring the boy here to me." Jesus rebuked the demon, and it came out of the boy, and he was healed at that moment.

Then the disciples came to Jesus in private and asked, "Why couldn't we drive it out?"

He replied, "Because you have so little faith. Truly I tell you, if you have faith as small as a mustard seed, you can say to this mountain, 'Move from here to there,' and it will move. Nothing will be impossible for you."

—Matthew 17:14–20 (NIV)

Did you notice that Jesus did not say the problem was with the demon? He did not say, "That is because they do not always come out." The problem was that their faith was too small. He told them, *"If you have faith as small as a mustard seed ... Nothing will be impossible for you"* (Matthew 17:20, NIV).

It seems some Christians think that what Jesus actually said was, "And nothing will be impossible for your pastor."

Many of us were raised in America with church viewed as a spectator sport. We had church on the calendar as an *event*—instead of understanding that *we* are the church.

The American church model, for the most part, is to hire and pay clergy to do all the work of the church. For example, if someone in the congregation is in the hospital, we would expect the pastor or another church staff member to go and see them.

But that is not the way the New Testament says the church should work. Paul says that Jesus gave the church its pastors, teachers, apostles, prophets, and evangelists to equip the *church members* for works of service. (See Ephesians 4:11–16).

According to the Bible, the pastor's job is not to be a superhero. The pastor is supposed to make the members of the congregation the superheroes.

So what Jesus is saying to *you* as a believer and a member of the church is that all things are possible for *you*.

There are offices in the church, of course, and people are called to those offices and step into the anointing by faith. But Jesus sent the church out to lay hands on the sick, and they shall recover.

We have to keep the concept of this spectator sport out of our minds. The people are the church. The building is not the church; that is just where the people gather. And so all things are possible for the people of the church.

This father had brought his son to the disciples, and they could not cast the demon out. We need to be spiritual scientists, and we need to know why. The stories in the Bible are not there for us to applaud Jesus for being so awesome. The point is not, "Oh, if only Jesus would show up, He would fix the problem!" That might be what other people think, but we have the stories in the Bible to show us how the Kingdom of God operates so that *we* can walk in it.

When we read a story like this, we need to ask questions. The disciples understood this. So, they asked, "Why were we unable to cast this demon out?"

We need to be asking the same thing in our lives. "Why did this happen?" "Why did this not happen?" We need to ask these questions because we are spiritual scientists. We understand that the Kingdom operates on laws. It is not a *feeling* issue; it is a *legal* issue.

Your salvation is a legal issue. It does not matter if you feel saved today or not. If you have called on the name of Jesus, legally, you are saved. When I was growing up, I did not always feel saved. I went to the altar to get saved probably 50 times. I did not understand that it was a legal issue.

In this story, the father said to Jesus, "Have mercy on my son. He has seizures. He suffers greatly. He falls into the fire and the water." So, what was happening there? The father was asking for mercy because that was all that was left.

If there is no legal right, no legal stance, no authority in a situation, all you have left is begging. But mercy implies that someone has the power to do something, and they just need to be convinced to act on your behalf.

That is why the father made the story so dramatic. He wanted to gain emotional favor with Jesus. "He has seizures. He falls into the fire." This father was dramatizing his kid's plight because he was trying to get Jesus to understand that this was a serious issue. He wanted Him to know how bad it really was.

You may have noticed that this is how most of the church prays, "Oh, God, you know I have got to have that big bill paid," and they start going through all the details. It is as though the longer they talk and the more details they give God, the greater the chance He will hear them. But Jesus told those who follow Him not to babble on like unbelievers when they pray (Matthew 6:7).

Jesus's response to those who babble on like this was: "*They think they will be heard because of their many words … your Father knows what you need before you ask him*" (Matthew 6:7b–8, NIV).

Jesus said, "*Lazarus, come out!*" (John 11:43, NIV). He did not begin with a whole lot of explanation. In fact, you will never see Jesus praying to the Father to take care of something. Jesus always exercised authority to deal with issues.

This father asked for mercy, and Jesus corrected him. "'*You unbelieving and perverse generation,' Jesus replied. 'How long shall I stay with you?*'" (Matthew 17:17a, NIV). Of course, Jesus then invited the boy to come to Him and immediately took care of the issue.

In this story, we see two things Jesus lists that give fear access to our lives—unbelief and perverse thinking. We need to address both of these issues if we want to stay free and understand our legal rights.

> *Do not be anxious about anything, but in every situation, by prayer and petition, with thanksgiving, present your requests to God. And the peace of God, which transcends all understanding, will guard your hearts and your minds in Christ Jesus.*
> —Philippians 4:6–7 (NIV)

"*Do not be anxious about anything*" reminds me of "*I will fear no evil*" (Psalm 23:4a, NIV). Anxiousness is fear. And the peace of God will guard our hearts from anxiousness—from fear. So, fear can have no place in our lives. We can say, "I am of the Kingdom of God. I am a son or daughter of God. I am a citizen. I have heaven's entire justice system to back up God's righteous living. I am not anxious about anything. Because it is done, I have thanksgiving."

I already shared some of my story, but I battled fear for quite a number of years. I was on antidepressants. I had panic attacks. I was acquainted with pawn shops. I lived a life of intense survival. We had babies to feed, and so we would dig our hands in the sofa cushions to find coins to buy a Happy Meal we could split among three kids. We just hoped the car would start. Everything we had was broken.

And as you can imagine, this is no way for anyone to live. When you live this way, you don't have a future. You can only live for today. You do not have vision because you do not have provision. You are just living. Well, you can call it that, but I call it hell on earth. Living in fear is hell on earth. It is living under the dominion of Satan. The Bible says fear is torment. And until I learned how the Kingdom operated, I was never free.

One thing I have learned is to never make a decision if you are anxious. This is because you are going to make the wrong one. You are going to make a "survival" decision instead of a "take territory" decision. Fear is irrational.

During that time, I was too afraid to leave my house. My life was very closed in. If you have ever dealt with serious fear issues, you know it is like a blanket that just hangs over your life. Thoughts that you do not want to think constantly flow through your mind. You are constantly thinking of all the bad things that could happen—the worst scenarios and the worst situations.

One time, I had a tooth problem, but we did not have any money to deal with it. So it got worse and worse. Eventually, my face started to swell up, and I had no other option but to get it fixed. It was an abscess in my tooth. I did not have the money, so I went to a local dental school because the students would do dental work for free as practice. Of course, they have teachers who oversee the students, and they do a great job.

But my jaw was so swollen and infected that it took days for the antibiotics to clear everything out. I was in pain during that time and could not sleep, so I was taking

Tylenol around the clock. I would get up and take it every four hours because I needed it for the pain. On the third day, after two and a half days of taking Tylenol, I was sitting downstairs at three o'clock in the morning looking at the bottle, and I saw the words, "Quick medical attention is critical."

So, I looked closer. There were the usual sentences about adults and children, normal signs and symptoms, and all the stuff you might expect, but the next sentence said, "Do not take more than directed." Okay, I got that. Then it said, "Adults and children twelve years and over, take two caplets every six hours."

So, I did the math. I had taken eight tablets in 24 hours.

The next sentence said, "Do not take more than six capsules in 24 hours."

I realized I had been taking two tablets too many for two and a half days.

"Quick medical attention is critical."

Fear immediately took hold.

"Quick."

"Critical."

"I am in trouble!"

So, I called the poison control center. It was three o'clock in the morning. We raised a bunch of kids, but this was the first time I had ever called them.

The lady answered, and I told her, "I took two tablets too many for two days."

"Okay, Mr. Keesee," she said. "What is your address?"

She took some information, and I heard her typing. And then this is exactly what she said, "Mr. Keesee, we have never had someone live that has taken that dosage."

Now, if you are battling fear, one thing you do not want to hear the expert at the poison control center say is, "Mr. Keesee, we have never had someone live that has taken that dosage."

"What?" I said, "Wait a minute." And I explained again that I only took two tablets more than it said on the label.

"I know, Mr. Keesee," she said. "You have a choice. You need to go to the hospital immediately. You can either drive yourself there, or I will send an ambulance for you right now."

I had to tell Drenda. She should know she was about to lose her husband. I was afraid to leave the house. We had no money. This was not good.

So, I went upstairs to the bedroom to wake her up.

"Drenda, I have overdosed on Tylenol. The poison control center says I have got to go to the hospital. They said I am dying."

I can still see her face today. She rolled her eyes. "Oh brother, Gary," she said. "If it is so deadly that two extra tablets will kill you, they are not going to sell Tylenol over the counter. Think about it. It is not going to kill you."

"I have to go to the hospital," I told her. "The expert said I am dying."

When I arrived at the emergency entrance of St. Ann's hospital, there were two guys in white coats pacing. They ran over to me. "Are you Mr. Keesee?" They took me straight in.

Normally, when you go into the hospital, you stop by a desk to give them all your information, but we rushed right by the desk to the little curtained room where the doctors meet with you.

I saw my name on the blackboard: *"Keesee, overdose."*

I have never taken drugs in my life, but now if you look up my medical history, I am a druggie who overdosed.

They took some blood. Then a few minutes later, the doctor came in and said, "Why are you here?"

I said, "Because I am dying. I took two too many Tylenol tablets."

He says, "You do not have enough Tylenol in your bloodstream to cure a headache."

I said, "I called poison control, and they said they have never had someone live that has taken that dosage."

The doctor doubled over laughing. He thought that was the funniest thing he had ever heard.

I was not laughing. And I ended up getting an emergency bill for over $2,000.

I share this story with you because if you allow fear to take your life and move you in different directions, it is going to take you on a trip you do not want to go on. It is going to take you down a road you do not want to go down and make you pay for it at the same time.

Jesus told us two things that will allow fear to enter your life: unbelief and perverse thinking.

Unbelief means there is no faith there. In the Bible, we see faith defined as *"being fully persuaded that God had power to do what he had promised"* (Romans 4:21, NIV). So, faith is being fully persuaded of what God says. Ephesians 6:16 says, *"Take up the shield of faith, with which you can extinguish all the flaming arrows of the evil one"* (Ephesians 6:16, NIV). If something comes at you that counters what God says or is not in alignment with His Word, it will be quenched and bounce off of your shield of faith like water off a duck's back. Fully persuaded means that you believe it completely.

I learned several years ago that Binney & Smith, the founders of the Crayola Crayon Company, decided to change the names of some of their colors for various reasons. If you were to look in the sky, you would see many colors. You would see a variety of blues, of course, and at times even reds and purples. But the company thought "sky blue" sounded best, so that is what they called that color, and then they put their crayons in the hands of the kids in kindergarten.[1]

But if someone handed you a crayon labeled "fuchsia," you might call it pink, purple, or even red, but you would be fully persuaded that it was not navy or royal blue or midnight blue.

Or if someone told you that you better grab something and hold on tight because they read on the Internet that gravity was about to be suspended in three minutes, would you be worried about it? Or are you fully persuaded that gravity exists and that it is not going away anytime soon?

---

[1] https://www.crayola.com/about-us/company/-/media/Crayola/About%20Us/History/Colorful%20Moments%20in%20Time_2023_102.pdf

That is what faith feels like. You are completely convinced that something is true.

And in the same way, when you are fully persuaded of what God says, you feel fully persuaded. The thought of believing anything else seems ridiculous.

If the doctor says, "You are going to die of cancer," that will be the craziest thing you will have heard all day. You will not believe him. If your business manager says, "You are going to go bankrupt," that will seem nuts to you. It won't make any sense at all.

When you are fully persuaded, you will reject ideas like this before they even have a chance to enter into your emotional thought process. They will just bounce off of you.

This is what faith feels like and what faith sounds like. And so you see, there are a lot of people in this world who simply are not in faith.

CHAPTER FIVE

JUST TELL IT TO LEAVE.

In Mark 4, there are three stories that explain what it will take to fully convince your heart and how your heart will become fully persuaded. In fact, Jesus said that this chapter of Mark is the most important chapter in the Bible.

"Then Jesus said to them, 'Don't you understand this parable? How then will you understand any parable?'" (Mark 4:13, NIV).

In other words, Jesus was saying, "If you do not know what I am talking about in this chapter, then you will not understand any other chapter."

We have to know how faith comes and how we become fully persuaded, because heaven can only invade Earth if a man or a woman's heart is fully persuaded. Your heart is the interface between heaven and Earth. You have legal jurisdiction here. Heaven cannot invade Earth unless someone like you, who has legal access in the earthly realm and is living on Earth, gives entrance into the earth realm for heaven's authority to flow. This is what we call faith.

Faith is always necessary on Earth. The reason that Jesus

could not heal in Nazareth was because their unbelief short-circuited the Kingdom. There were no fully persuaded hearts there (Mark 6:5–6). Faith is required to make the connection between heaven and Earth.

The first of these three stories tells us how to bring this agreement. We need to learn the laws of the Kingdom because our hearts were trained wrong. This is because we grew up in the valley of the shadow of death.

We grew up thinking that certain things produce certain things, and we are very confident about this. If we want to make any kind of change, we have to reprogram our hearts. If we want to be free from fear, Jesus told us that we must reprogram our thinking to come into alignment with what God says.

> *This is what the kingdom of God is like. A man scatters seed on the ground. Night and day, whether he sleeps or gets up, the seed sprouts and grows, though he does not know how. All by itself the soil produces grain—first the stalk, then the head, then the full kernel in the head. As soon as the grain is ripe, he puts the sickle to it, because the harvest has come.*
>
> —Mark 4:26–29 (NIV)

In an earlier parable, Jesus explained to His disciples that the "seed" is the Word of God, and the "ground" is the heart of man. And so we see that Jesus was talking about how faith is produced, which would be the "ripe" grain.

Jesus was using an agricultural illustration. If you plant a soybean seed in the ground, the soybean plant begins to grow. Eventually, it produces soybeans, and eventually, they ripen. Once they are ripe, the seed—the new soybeans—matches the seed initially sown in the ground.

Heaven wants to bring the will of God into the earthly realm but has no jurisdiction to do so. So, it has to go through a man or woman who has legal authority in the earthly realm. So, God puts the Word of God into the heart of a man or woman, where it begins to incubate. And all by itself, the Word in your heart begins to ripen and produce agreement with heaven.

So, night or day, whether you sleep or get up, you do not know how it happens, but your spirit begins to produce agreement. When that agreement is there, your heart will reflect the same picture as the picture in heaven. They will look identical.

If you are sick, the picture in heaven shows you are healed. So when you are in faith, you will see yourself healed. This does not mean you are mentally trying to tell yourself that you are healed, but rather you will see yourself healed. You will know you are healed.

So many people try to see it for themselves, but that is not the solution. What they have to do is change their heart picture on the inside.

> *What shall we say the kingdom of God is like, or what parable shall we use to describe it? It is like a mustard seed, which is the smallest of all seeds on earth. Yet when planted, it grows and becomes the largest of all garden plants, with such big branches that the birds can perch in its shade.*
>
> —Mark 4:30–32 (NIV)

The next story gives us a clearer picture of what the Kingdom is like. We have this garden—our hearts—full of all kinds of ideas and the perverse thoughts we learned in the earthly realm (cancer equals death, divorce, poverty, bankruptcy, etc.).

So you have all these ideas that you learned in the earthly realm—the kingdom of fear—and you have spent your life building all kinds of defense mechanisms to protect you from all these things. And now the Bible says, using an example of the smallest seed, that when you put that small seed in the garden, it begins to grow. Before long, it becomes the largest plant in the garden, so big that even birds can rest in its shade. (If you have never seen a mustard seed, it is about the size of a grain of sand.)

Once that mustard seed has grown into the largest tree in the garden, when you look at the garden, all you can see is the tree. And when faith is there, that is all you can see. It shades out every weed, and it takes over the garden.

It is the same with the Word of God. You put the Word of God in your heart, and all by itself, it will begin to grow. You will not know how, but day or night, sleep or awake, all by itself, it will grow. Our spirits have been created to incubate and produce agreement with the Word of God.

But now, here is the dangerous part.

This will work for anything you put in your heart. Fear is being fully persuaded of alternative facts. That is why the Bible warns us, *"Above all else, guard your heart, for everything you do flows from it"* (Proverbs 4:23, NIV). We must guard our hearts above everything else because Satan is trying to pollute our hearts above everything else.

The enemy knows how the human spirit operates. He knows that if he can snag your attention and get you to begin to meditate on something else, all by itself, day or night, whether you sleep or get up, you will find that thing growing. And pretty soon, you will become like the mustard seed. At first, you think you can handle it and tell yourself, "Just once will not hurt." But it grows and soon becomes a problem, and you are enslaved by that one little thought. And you find yourself in bondage.

This is why you have to understand that when you sow a seed into your spirit, it will grow and manifest. This is how the human spirit is made. Believe me, you do not want full-grown trees of wrong thoughts in there!

You do not want to pick up those stray thoughts. You need to cast those thoughts down. You counter them with the shield of faith and the Word of God. You only say what God says.

But if you do not know these truths, even if you are born again and going to heaven, you are going to live like an unbeliever. You are going to have the same fruit as an unbeliever. Until you learn who you are, what is legally yours, and how to handle it, you will have the same results as anyone else. You will live an enslaved life, and slaves cannot set slaves free. You need to be free if you want to help others be free. So, you need to know your legal rights.

In the book of Acts, we see that Paul knew his rights as a Roman citizen, and he boldly stood on them, both in Philippi and then later in Jerusalem.

> *When it was daylight, the magistrates sent their officers to the jailer with the order: "Release those men." The jailer told Paul, "The magistrates have ordered that you and Silas be released. Now you can leave. Go in peace."*
>
> *But Paul said to the officers: "They beat us publicly without a trial, even though we are Roman citizens, and threw us into prison. And now do they want to get rid of us quietly? No! Let them come themselves and escort us out."*

The officers reported this to the magistrates, and when they heard that Paul and Silas were Roman citizens, they were alarmed. They came to appease them and escorted them from the prison."

—Acts 16:35–39a (NIV)

The commander ordered that Paul be taken into the barracks. He directed that he be flogged and interrogated in order to find out why the people were shouting at him like this. As they stretched him out to flog him, Paul said to the centurion standing there, "Is it legal for you to flog a Roman citizen who hasn't even been found guilty?"

When the centurion heard this, he went to the commander and reported it. "What are you going to do?" he asked. "This man is a Roman citizen."

The commander went to Paul and asked, "Tell me, are you a Roman citizen?"

"Yes, I am," he answered.

Then the commander said, "I had to pay a lot of money for my citizenship."

"But I was born a citizen," Paul replied.

Those who were about to interrogate him withdrew immediately. The commander himself was alarmed when he realized that he had put Paul, a Roman citizen, in chains.

—Acts 22:24–29 (NIV)

The Bible says, "*Submit yourselves, then, to God. Resist the devil, and he will flee from you*" (James 4:7, NIV). The word "flee" here means to run away in terror.

When the magistrates heard that Paul and Silas were Roman citizens, they were *alarmed* and came to appease them and escort them from the prison.

When the commander learned that Paul was a Roman citizen, he was *alarmed* and withdrew immediately.

If you do not know your legal rights, then you will accept flogging as though it is God's will for you.

The devil will always try to take you down a road you do not want. And you do not know any better because you have never been taught that you do not have to go down that road. As I said, we have been raised in a perverse generation. So, you actually learned to think wrong. You believe that God allows these things. "Well, God knows best. He is teaching me through these floggings."

Think about that for a minute. You are not guilty. Your citizenship is in heaven. You did not pay for it. You were born into that government. Satan has no jurisdiction over you. He cannot tie you up. He cannot flog you. He cannot throw sickness on you. He has zero jurisdiction over you (unless you lie down and say, "Go ahead, flog me").

So instead, you need to be like Paul. "Excuse me! What you are doing is not legal, so back off!" And just as we saw in Paul's situation, the enemy will back off immediately.

It is amazing to me that most believers do not know this. I travel a lot, and it is my observation that the majority of churches believe that God allows bad things to happen, that God does bad things, and that God thinks that is best.

They are not aware of the fact that God gave us the keys to the Kingdom. They do not know that in the earthly realm, we have legal jurisdiction. But if we do not bind, it is not bound. If we do not loose, it is not loosed.

Satan wants to teach you and train you with a perverse understanding.

Recently, I read about a woman who had been killed in an accident. This was a very horrible thing, of course. But these are the words her husband posted on Facebook:

> "She was an amazing person. I miss her like crazy. I will never get over this. We were supposed to live our lives out together, with lines on our faces from a lifetime of smiles. We were supposed to grow old and laugh, and talk about times gone by. But my pastor said on Sunday morning that my wife was only on loan to me. She always belonged to God, and He needed this beautiful angel in heaven and called her to her heavenly home."

My friend, that is as perverse as you can get! Was that man's pastor saying that God chose to take his wife home? If that were true, who would want to serve that God?

How would we know when to fight something? We might think, *Maybe that cancer is God's will. Maybe that divorce is God's will.* How would we know what was right and wrong? This is a perverse understanding of life. You live in fear because you think fear is normal. And you fear God because you never know what He is going to throw at you next.

This is why we need an understanding of who we are legally. We have to know the Word of God. We have to talk back to fear when it comes at us.

When I was very sick, I began to read as much as I could, because I knew nothing about the Kingdom. I began to read and read and read because I was in really bad shape. I read the stories of the Bible. I read other people's stories. Slowly, hope began to build inside of me. I began to catch the authority I had. I began to understand the Kingdom, and I began to get a little better.

But I could not get fear off my back even though I would say, "In the name of Jesus." Fear still would not react because I was not in faith. Fear did not have to leave because I had no jurisdiction. Heaven had no jurisdiction because I was not in faith. I was in fear. But as I began to read the Word of God, my faith began to emerge, and things began to change.

One day at the office, I had a particularly bad morning. If you have ever battled serious, tormenting fear, you know it is an awful feeling. It takes over all your thoughts.

I was praying, and the Lord spoke to me and said, "Tell it to leave."

"Here is what you need to do," He said. "You tell it to leave, but pay no attention to your emotions because they have no bearing on this story. You tell it to leave and believe that it will leave because my Word says so. Pay no attention to the result. Pay no attention to if fear reacts or not. Pay no attention to anything. But keep your mind and your eyes on my Word, and then thank Me that it has been dealt with."

I was in my little one-man office, and I knew that I needed to deal with this. I knew that it would not be a quiet, little, "Father, I come to you…" prayer. I had to get serious! It was going to be more of a loud, powerful, "In the Name of Jesus" prayer! And because there were other people working around me who would think I was nuts for screaming at the devil from my office, I went into the restroom.

When I got alone, I said, "In the name of Jesus, I bind you, you foul spirit. Fear, I command you to leave me now. According to the Word of God, this is illegal, and I take authority over you. I am free, in Jesus's name. Go!"

I felt nothing. Nothing changed. I still felt bad. But I remembered God said, "Pay no attention." So I said, "Thank you, Father. I thank you that I am free. I thank you that I am free. I thank you that I am free, Father."

Then, I went back to my desk. I just sat there and praised the Lord for a few minutes. About 20 minutes after I had sat down, I suddenly began to shake. The Holy Spirit came into that room. I began to shake under the power of the Holy Spirit, I saw a black, wispy mist go up right through the ceiling—and I was free.

Talk about a good day; that was a good day! I was so excited. I was excited because I then knew how to handle fear. I called Drenda and said, "Guess what? I learned how to deal with this thing and win over it in the name of Jesus!" I said, "We have got to celebrate. We have got to have some Chinese food!" So, we went to the Chinese restaurant, and we had a party!

Now, that thing tried to come back many times. But every time it did, I just did the same thing again, and it would leave. So maybe the first week, it tried to come back twenty times. The second week, maybe ten times. The third week, maybe five times. Then maybe once a month, then twice a year, and now it does not come back at all.

The devil backs off when he knows we know who we are and we know the authority we have. He just goes to find someone else. But at first, he tries to spook us to see if we will back up when we receive some kind of stimulus that puts the thought back in our minds that this might be bigger than God.

> *This is the confidence we have in approaching God: that if we ask anything according to his will, he hears us. And if we know that he hears us—whatever we ask—we know that we have what we asked of him.*
> —1 John 5:14–15 (NIV)

I get emails all the time from people who ask me why faith is not working for them. But the fact that they are asking the question answers the question. What is faith? Faith is being fully persuaded. They are not healed because they are not fully persuaded. They are in unbelief. We have to know how it works.

But there is a remedy for that. You can get faith, because faith comes by the Word of God. You need to learn how to read yourself to see if you are in faith or not. Then, if you are not in faith, you need to become a really good attorney for yourself. This is a legal issue. The laws are clear on the matter. You do not need to beg anyone for anything. Your issue is that you do not know how to legally bring it to bear and manifest it in your life, not that you do not have it. The case has already been decided by the Judge. You have already been set free.

CHAPTER SIX

THE GOODNESS OF THE FATHER

According to the folks at Google, the top three searches for questions about God are as follows:

#1 - "Who created God?"

This is the number one search on the Internet about God, and of course, the Bible is clear. God was not created. It says He has no beginning and no end. When you get to heaven, you can ask Him exactly how this all works, but the Bible does say that He has no beginning and no end.

#2 - "Why does God allow suffering?"

This is an important question, of course, but the short answer is that God is not the source of suffering. The Bible says that every good and perfect gift comes from God, and there is no variableness or change in Him. He is the same yesterday, today, and forever. God does not allow evil, and He does not tempt you with evil. Adam is the one who rebelled against God and gave Satan access to the earthly realm. And Satan is the thief. He is the one who comes to kill, steal, and destroy.

But the third question is where I want to focus now.

#3 - "Why does God hate me?"

We need to address this issue. In a way, it touches on the second question because if you believe that God does bad things to good people, then you will have trouble believing that God cares for you.

> *"Let us then approach God's throne of grace with confidence, so that we may receive mercy and find grace to help us in our time of need."*
>
> —Hebrews 4:16, NIV)

Grace is God's power, your answer in your time of need. I believe that people have trouble approaching God with confidence because when they come before God, they bring themselves with them.

So many people, even Christians, believe God is disappointed with them. This is because they filter their image of themselves and God through themselves. When they come to approach God, they start thinking: *I have not prayed enough. I have not done enough. I have not fasted. I have not read my Bible today. I am not spiritual enough. God is not happy with me. In fact, He is disappointed with me.* And so every time they come to God, they judge themselves as unworthy and have no confidence.

This happens to a lot of Christians because of the religious training they have received, and it goes back to the beginning with Adam and Eve.

The woman ... saw that the tree was beautiful and its fruit looked delicious, and she wanted the wisdom it would give her. So she took some of the fruit and ate it.

Then she gave some to her husband, who was with her, and he ate it, too. At that moment their eyes were opened, and they suddenly felt shame at their nakedness. So they sewed fig leaves together to cover themselves.

When the cool evening breezes were blowing, the man and his wife heard the Lord God walking about in the garden. So they hid from the Lord God among the trees.

Then the Lord God called to the man, "Where are you?"

He replied, "I heard you walking in the garden, so I hid. I was afraid because I was naked."

—Genesis 3:6–10 (NLT)

I do not believe the term "naked" is really talking about having no clothes on. Adam and Eve, of course, were cloaked with the Holy Spirit. They were filled with the Spirit of God, and when Adam kicked God out—when he rebelled against God—I believe there was an instant void.

I believe it was the shame and guilt that made them feel exposed and naked. They were always naked. It was the sudden guilt and shame that made them afraid of God.

Since that day, people have been sewing fig leaves and covering themselves with them. Although we may not use actual fig leaves, people are still trying to cover themselves in materialism, identity, and position. They are still trying to cover their lack. They are still trying to cover their nakedness to make themselves feel worthy and see themselves as valuable. Until you fix that in your life, you will have a hard time receiving from God. You will always judge yourself as lacking and coming up short.

Religion has taught us dos and don'ts. *If you are a Christian, you cannot do this. Christians always have to do that.* It is all tied to the things we do.

This is why people in the earthly realm ask, "Who are you?" And we typically answer with what we do. This is because since Adam became a survivalist and tried to find his own identity, in the earthly realm, people have been judging everyone by what they do. So, we answer, "Well, I am a salesman" or "I manage a store." But who we are is important.

When I was a child, we had a pony named Tony. We did not have a barn at our house, so we kept him at Grandpa's barn, which was about half a mile away from our house. Every day, I would ride my bike over to water and feed Tony, the pony.

One day, I took a friend from school with me, and we went over to feed Tony. We were in fourth grade and did not understand some things about life, like why there was a big stack of storm windows just sitting there.

We did not have storm windows in our house. I thought they were just old windows. But these were the storm windows Grandma and Grandpa used in their 1850s house to protect themselves from the winter. Well, for some reason, we decided to break every one of them.

Then, we noticed boxes and boxes of canning jars. My grandparents were farmers, so they canned, but mom did not, so I did not understand what they were. They looked like old jars. We broke every single one of Grandma's canning jars.

We also noticed a few boxes of light bulbs. We broke every one of them. And then, we broke all the windows out of the barn and broke the windows out of my grandpa's truck.

To this day, I do not know why I did that. I loved my grandpa. But when the fun was over, I realized that it was not good.

Fear came over me.

I did not want to see my grandpa at that moment.

I did not want to see my dad at that moment.

I wanted to hide.

And my relationship with my grandpa was injured then because I did not want to see my grandpa, who loved me very much.

I rode the school bus to school. Coming home two days later, I saw my grandpa's car in our driveway through the school bus window. I can still remember the wave of fear that came over me.

Now, they did not know exactly who broke the windows. It could have been a vandal. Anyone could have done it. They could not have known.

My grandpa looked me in the eye. He said, "Did you break the windows in the barn?"

I said, "Yes."

At that moment, the fear left me. How did I get rid of the fear? I confessed.

There were consequences, but the relationship was restored.

Otherwise, I would have been hiding for a long, long time.

This is how it is with people and God. They know they have blown it. They know they come up short. They hang back. They do not come to God in confidence because they do not have confidence in themselves. They do not feel they are spiritual enough, and so they hang back. They still have hope, but they hang back.

Until you fix this, however, the bottom line is that you are going to have trouble receiving from God.

> *Let us then approach God's throne of grace with confidence, so that we may receive mercy and find grace to help us in our time of need.*
> —Hebrews 4:16 (NIV)

Perhaps the best story in the Bible to illustrate this is known as the "Prodigal Son" from Luke 15:11–32. I believe it is misnamed, however. It is not really about the son. It is the story of the loving father.

> *There was a man who had two sons. The younger one said to his father, "Father, give me my share of the estate." So he divided his property between them.*
> —Luke 15:11–12 (NIV)

First of all, we need to keep in mind that this story is an analogy. Jesus was referring back to the day that Adam, who had it all in the Father's house, made the decision to leave, thinking that there were greener pastures somewhere else. So, the younger son is Adam in this story.

> *Not long after that, the younger son got together all he had, set off for a distant country and there squandered his wealth in wild living. After he had spent everything, there was a severe famine in that whole country, and he began to be in need.*
> —Luke 15:13–14 (NIV)

There was a severe famine in the entire country. When Adam left God's house—kicking God out of the earthly realm—he came under the jurisdiction of Satan. And before long, Adam found himself in an impoverished kingdom, a kingdom of poverty, sickness, disease, and fear. And he began to experience need.

> *So he went and hired himself out to a citizen of that country, who sent him to his fields to feed pigs.*
> —Luke 15:15 (NIV)

This was the first time this son ever found himself in need, because he had come from a very wealthy home and had a father who loved him. So then to survive, he became a hireling. Before this, his life was all about *who* he was, not *what* he did. But then, his goal was to survive.

Jesus was telling this story to Jews, who considered pigs to be unclean. This occupation was about the worst that those Jews could have imagined.

> *He longed to fill his stomach with the pods that the pigs were eating, but no one gave him anything.*
> —Luke 15:16 (NIV)

The son was in the pigsty, and no one was going to hand him anything. Everyone around him was also trying to survive. He was in the valley of the shadow of death, which means the stench of death. He was in survival mode.

> *When he came to his senses, he said, "How many of my father's hired servants have food to spare, and here I am starving to death! I will set out and go back to my father and say to him: 'Father, I have sinned against heaven and against you. I am no longer worthy to be called your son; make me like one of your hired servants.'"*
> —Luke 15:17–19 (NIV)

This son had a memory of his father's goodness, but you do not because you grew up in this valley of the shadow of death, in the survival realm, in the earthly realm that Adam brought under Satan's dominion.

This is why God sends people to preach His goodness to you. It is so you can hear about His goodness, because you do not have a memory of His goodness.

> *So he got up and went to his father. But while he was still a long way off, his father saw him and was filled with compassion for him; he ran to his son, threw his arms around him and kissed him.*
>
> —Luke 15:20 (NIV)

Do you know what happened to the father the minute he did that? He became unclean—because the son was unclean, covered with the filth of the pigsty. When the father willingly took upon himself the stench of the pigsty, he willingly made himself unclean on behalf of the son as he kissed him.

> *The son said to him, "Father, I have sinned against heaven and against you. I am no longer worthy to be called your son."*

> *But the father said to his servants, "Quick! Bring the best robe and put it on him. Put a ring on his finger and sandals on his feet. Bring the fattened calf and kill it. Let's have a feast and celebrate. For this son of mine was dead and is alive again; he was lost and is found."*
>
> —Luke 15:21–24a (NIV)

The father took it upon himself to cover the son's sin, to cover his mistake, and to cover the stench. He took it upon himself to cover his son with the best robe. The ring he put on his finger was the family signet ring, so he was reinstating the authority the son had over the kingdom. When the father gave him the sandals, he was essentially giving him the entire kingdom. In those days in Israel, for whatever reason, when they bought real estate, they exchanged sandals. (You can read about this in Ruth 4:7). So everything in the kingdom was then at the son's disposal. When the father gave his son the fatted calf, that meant he had received the prosperity of the kingdom.

> *So they began to celebrate.*
>
> —Luke 15:24b (NIV)

When people come to Christ, they are born again, and they understand God's love. But when they come to God, they often bring something with them. They bring the "hireling" mentality they learned back in the earthly realm.

They feel they have to perform to be accepted. They believe they have to "do" to justify themselves. So even though they are in church, even though they know that God loves them, they carry this attitude with them. They carry this hireling mentality with them back into church because they believe the problem is with them. And they often come in with an "I want to work for God" instinct.

But believe me, you do not want to work *for* God. You want to work *with* God. Until you change your mentality, you will always judge yourself and come up short. You can never work enough to feel as though you have done enough to approach God with confidence.

So, you have to be changed. You have to change your thinking to understand who you are. In the parable, it was really the father's choice. The son had nothing to do with it. The father took it upon himself to cover his son with the robe. God is the father in this story, and He takes upon Himself our errors, our weaknesses, our mistakes. He covers us. He gives us back the authority. He gives us back the estate. He gives us the wealth of the Kingdom.

Here is one more little side note: In Jewish culture, the oldest son would get the double portion of the father's inheritance. The younger son had done nothing to deserve more because he had already taken his share. He had already taken his half of the estate. But the father restored him to full standing as a son, so he would then enjoy a second portion that he did not deserve.

> *Meanwhile, the older son was in the field. When he came near the house, he heard music and dancing. So he called one of the servants and asked him what was going on. "Your brother has come," he replied, "and your father has killed the fattened calf because he has him back safe and sound." The older brother became angry and refused to go in.*
> —Luke 15:25–28a (NIV)

The older brother was angry because in the earthly realm, we have been trained that everything is based on what we *do*, not who we *are*. We will always have a hard time receiving until we understand that we deserve it not because of what *we do* but because of what the *Father did.* We find it hard to be confident before God, because we have a filter between us and God that causes us to judge ourselves and say, "You have not done enough. You have to do more so that God is happy with you."

> So his father went out and pleaded with him. But he answered his father, "Look! All these years I've been slaving for you and never disobeyed your orders. Yet you never gave me even a young goat so I could celebrate with my friends. But when this son of yours who has squandered your property with prostitutes comes home, you kill the fattened calf for him!"
>
> —Luke 15:28b–30 (NIV)

The older brother had the wrong perspective of his father. He thought he had to slave for his father. He thought he had to work hard to please his father. So then his brother came back. He had done nothing to deserve what he received, but his father had given him back everything. On top of that, his portion of the inheritance was restored—taken from the double portion, which belonged to the older son, who thought he could earn everything.

"My son," the father said, "you are always with me, and everything I have is yours. But we had to celebrate and be glad, because this brother of yours was dead and is alive again; he was lost and is found."

—Luke 15:31–32 (NIV)

Friend, we need to get this straightened out. The older brother was so busy working for his father that he never got to enjoy his relationship with his father—because he thought he always had to be working to please his father.

I believe many Christians have this same mindset. "Make me like a hired servant. I will earn my self-righteousness. I will earn, I will work, and you will be proud of me!"

But they are missing the whole point. We do not have to earn it. We already have it.

You do not have to hide from God. In fact, you cannot hide. Nothing good happens in hiding. When you hide, you stay out of the loop, you stay out of the blessing, and you stay out of what God has for you.

When you stay in the devil's territory, know that he is going to torment you with that forever until you deal with it.

But praise God, you already have the entire Kingdom! You have the authority of the Kingdom. The Bible says you are a co-heir with Christ—so everything that Jesus has, you already have. You do not have to beg for anything. You just need to know who you are, and you need to relax. You need to be able to receive. You already have the prosperity of the Kingdom. You are already righteous and perfect in God's sight through Jesus Christ.

> *In him and through faith in him we may approach God with freedom and confidence.*
> —Ephesians 3:12 (NIV)

You simply need to change your thinking to be able to receive. Because if you believe that God is not happy with you, then you will not hang out with Him. You are not going to learn how the Kingdom operates. You are not going to figure out who you are in Christ. And you certainly will not believe that you will receive when you pray.

There is no fear in love. But perfect love drives out fear, because fear has to do with punishment. The one who fears is not made perfect in love.

—1 John 4:18 (NIV)

That is powerful: "*Fear has to do with punishment. The one who fears has not been made perfect in love.*" Fortunately, God has shown us what love looks like in the story of the Prodigal Son. He has chosen to do that for you.

That is exactly what God wants for you today. He wants you to be confident and at ease in His presence, to know who you are in Christ, what you have in Christ, and to enjoy that relationship as He does.

You need to live this way every day. You can live in God's presence with the confidence that there is nothing against you, that He is for you, that you can walk right in there and say, "Pass the biscuits" and "Pass the jelly" because it is your house. It is your Kingdom. You are part of God's household, and because of that, you have everything. God wants you to know He is not holding anything against you.

The good news is that the Father took it upon Himself to make you perfect. You could never do that. He took it upon Himself to call you perfect and to take the stench of mistakes and weaknesses away from you. You'll still have to cast those thoughts down because we are human and we do make mistakes, but the Bible says you have an advocate with the Father, Jesus Christ. When we make a mistake, the Bible says we can confess it, and *"he is faithful and just and will forgive us our sins and purify us from all unrighteousness"* (1 John 1:9, NIV). Have you ever taken a nice hot shower after working hard in the yard all day? It is a great feeling!

CHAPTER SEVEN

OUR GREATEST FEAR

What would you guess is the greatest fear of mankind? Many people might guess death. But death is actually number five on the list.

It turns out humankind's greatest fear is public speaking.

If you ask someone to speak in front of a crowd, they are likely to say, "Shoot me!" first. People just do not want to be embarrassed, and they do not want to put themselves in situations where they feel insecure.

Let me paraphrase what this actually means: the fear of public speaking is basically the fear of people. The fear of people is the greatest fear we must overcome.

Every one of us has faced potentially embarrassing situations where we do not feel secure. We just do not feel great about having to make ourselves vulnerable.

I took piano lessons as a kid and played for several years; and as part of my training, I learned how to "sight read." But I had not done that for quite a few years when our family was invited to put on a little concert for a nursing home, and they asked me to play the piano for a few Christmas carols. I had not read music for a long time and was a little worried because it had been such a long time since I had played from a sheet of music. But I finally agreed, and we went down and gave them a little concert. At the end of my performance, I learned that it was a deaf nursing home.

So, all my fear was for naught. They did not hear a single note I played. Apparently, they could pick up the vibrations and tap their feet along with them, but they did not hear the piano.

A lot of the time, if not most of the time, the fear we have is not justified. When we find out what is really behind our fear, it's not like we thought it would be, which is good.

"Fear of man will prove to be a snare, but whoever trusts in the Lord is kept safe" (Proverbs 29:25, NIV).

Dictionary.com tells us that a snare is a device, often consisting of a noose, for entangling small game [like birds or mammals]. When something is entangled, where does it go? Nowhere. If a bird is caught in a snare, it is stuck and cannot go forward. It also cannot go backward.

When you get entangled in the snares of men, you cannot go anywhere either. *The Living Bible* says, "*Fear of man is a dangerous trap*" (Proverbs 29:25b). If fear has you entangled, you are probably trying to back up, play it safe, and hide from people—which means you are stuck. This is a problem because when you have a need that God wants to meet in your life, do you know how He is probably going to meet that need? Through people.

Unfortunately, walking in the fear of man will prove to be a snare. But it can be even more devastating than that. It can actually derail you and stop your progress toward your destiny. Your destiny is your God-breathed purpose in life, the place you are called to occupy. And the biggest issue is not so much about you and your destiny personally but about the people you are going to influence in your destiny.

God is in the people business. He loves people. And as believers, of course, we should love people too. But we also need to be wise. Satan will use people to try to stop us from God's plan for us and our lives.

You may know the story of Hannah in the Bible. She dedicated her son Samuel to the ministry at the

Tabernacle. The high priest at the time was Eli. But there was a problem.

> *Eli's sons were scoundrels; they had no regard for the Lord. Now it was the practice of the priests that, whenever any of the people offered a sacrifice, the priest's servant would come with a three-pronged fork in his hand while the meat was being boiled and would plunge the fork into the pan or kettle or caldron or pot. Whatever the fork brought up the priest would take for himself. This is how they treated all the Israelites who came to Shiloh. But even before the fat was burned, the priest's servant would come and say to the person who was sacrificing, "Give the priest some meat to roast; he won't accept boiled meat from you, but only raw."*

> *If the person said to him, "Let the fat be burned first, and then take whatever you want," the servant would answer, "No, hand it over now; if you don't, I'll take it by force."*

> *This sin of the young men was very great in the Lord's sight, for they were treating the Lord's offering with contempt ...*

Now Eli, who was very old, heard about everything his sons were doing to all Israel and how they slept with the women who served at the entrance to the tent of meeting. So he said to them, "Why do you do such things? I hear from all the people about these wicked deeds of yours. No, my sons; the report I hear spreading among the Lord's people is not good. If one person sins against another, God may mediate for the offender; but if anyone sins against the Lord, who will intercede for them?" His sons, however, did not listen to their father's rebuke …

Now a man of God came to Eli and said to him … "This is what the Lord says … 'Why do you scorn my sacrifice and offering that I prescribed for my dwelling? Why do you honor your sons more than me by fattening yourselves on the choice parts of every offering made by my people Israel?'

Therefore the Lord, the God of Israel, declares: 'I promised that members of your family would minister before me forever.' But now the Lord declares: 'Far be it from me! Those who honor me I will honor, but those who despise me will be disdained.'"

—1 Samuel 2:12–17; 22–25; 27a–30 (NIV)

How was Eli despising God? He was choosing people over God. The prophet told him that God will honor those who honor Him, but He cannot promote those who do not honor Him.

But Eli never dealt with his sons. Then Israel went into battle against the Philistines, and it did not go well. A messenger brought the news to Eli.

> *He told Eli, "I have just come from the battle line; I fled from it this very day."*
>
> *Eli asked, "What happened, my son?"*
>
> *The man who brought the news replied, "Israel fled before the Philistines, and the army has suffered heavy losses. Also your two sons, Hophni and Phinehas, are dead, and the ark of God has been captured."*
>
> *When he mentioned the ark of God, Eli fell backward off his chair by the side of the gate. His neck was broken and he died, for he was an old man, and he was heavy. He had led Israel forty years.*
>
> —1 Samuel 4:16–18 (NIV)

We can see in this story that there were a lot of problems. Israel was engaged in this physical battle because the nation was not in a good place spiritually. The high priest, Eli, was confronted and corrected by the prophet because he would not deal with people—in this case, his sons. It did not matter that they were his sons. Because he was spiritually in charge of the entire nation, he was responsible for dealing with all the people. It is important to recognize this because if you refuse to deal with people, God cannot use you in a greater assignment.

You are passing the test in your current area of responsibility every day if you are walking with truth, walking in righteousness, and walking with people. But if you choose to back off because people are intimidating you, then you are at risk of failing. You have to recognize that, at times, people will not always be your greatest cheerleaders and that Satan will use people (and their immaturity) against you whenever he can. But we do not serve people in the sense that they are our bosses. We honor God. So, you have to choose to honor God, no matter what happens with people around you. Whether they follow you or not, that is not your problem. You have to make a decision. God will honor you if you honor Him.

I have a Scripture taped to my laptop computer so that every time I open it, I read these words:

> *Hear me, you who know what is right, you people who have taken my instruction to heart: "Do not fear the reproach of mere mortals or be terrified by their insults."*
>
> —Isaiah 51:7 (NIV)

As a leader, I have to be focused. Yes, I take care of people; that is an important part of my assignment. But at the same time, I cannot let people dictate or intimidate me from following what God has for my life. I have to make a decision. And I choose to follow the Lord.

> *The Lord is my light and my salvation—whom shall I fear? The Lord is the stronghold of my life—of whom shall I be afraid?*
>
> —Psalm 27:1 (NIV)

We understand that Satan uses people to intimidate and stop your progress in life. We also know that God uses people to advance your situation.

Why was David promoted to king? Because he was not

afraid and took out Goliath. King Saul had the authority, but he backed away in fear and became disqualified.

Friend, you do not want to be disqualified. Yet, if you are entangled in the fear of man, you will possibly find yourself disqualified. God will just find someone else. He will find someone else who will say "Yes" to Him and who will not be moved by the opinions of other people. He will find people who trust Him. But as a follower of Jesus Christ, it should be you. You have to make a decision to follow hard after God.

The apostle Paul gave Timothy some noteworthy advice on how he should pick the leaders of the church.

> *Now the overseer is to be above reproach, faithful to his wife, temperate, self-controlled, respectable, hospitable, able to teach, not given to drunkenness, not violent but gentle, not quarrelsome, not a lover of money. He must manage his own family well and see that his children obey him, and he must do so in a manner worthy of full respect. (If anyone does not know how to manage his own family, how can he take care of God's church?).*
>
> —1 Timothy 3:2–5 (NIV)

If you are a parent, please pay close attention to this. How you train your children to respect authority and follow after God is vital. You are setting them on a path of either going after their destiny or living a life of being intimidated. If they decide that they are going to be in charge of their lives and choose what they want to do, then they are going to miss God.

How your children respond to the people they see is how they are going to respond to a God they do not see. If they will not obey a person in front of them, they will never obey God. It is crucial that they learn how authority operates, how discipline operates, and how to say "no" to themselves. They must have a bigger picture of their life than themselves. And as their parents, you must train your children for life. Once you take your hand off them, they will be governed by whatever is in their hearts—plus whatever you put in there.

We have all had to overcome fear in our lives, but in my particular case, it was pretty severe. I was paralyzed by fear growing up. In high school, I would sit in the back row of the class, dreading that the teacher would ask for people to volunteer comments. (I figured they would never see me if I hid in the back.) I never said anything. One day,

I was talking with a friend as we walked down the hall, and one of my teachers was behind me. She caught up and stopped me. "Hey, you can talk," she said. "I did not know you could talk." She had never heard me talk the entire school year. And that is how I lived.

I was on the high school football team, and when we played on Friday nights, we would have a party at our house. But I would go into my bedroom and shut the door because I did not want to be around all the people, and everyone else would have a party.

Looking back, I know I had a problem. But God is bigger than any of my issues. And He is bigger than yours. God can help you if you will allow Him, but you must choose to allow Him to do so.

When I was 19, I was called to preach through a vision. Obviously, God had to use a very dramatic calling for someone that shy, so I knew for a fact it was God.

But there still was a problem. This quiet kid, sitting in the back row, was called to preach the Gospel. Who was he going to preach to? Trees? How is God going to fix that?

God called me to go to college, so I had a choice to make. Was I going to live in that bedroom, lock the door, and let life pass me by my entire life while I looked out the window and watched other people live the good life? Or was I going to come out into the open?

I knew the only way to win over fear was to confront it. That is the only way. You face it, and you overcome it.

When God called me to college, it was the hardest thing I had ever done. It was probably the first thing I had ever done and the hardest thing I had ever done.

I do not remember much about high school because I was not there much. I remember fishing and playing hooky a lot. I do not know how many days I missed, but I think they were glad to get me out of there. I had a 1.3 grade point, and I am pretty sure I was not voted most likely to succeed.

So, for me, being consistent over four years in college was tough. I had to learn how to write. As a freshman, I wrote a paper, and my professor sent it back with a big red F on it. I was assigned a tutor to teach me how to write in the English language.

But I stayed. I persevered. And I finished.

Then God got to work on my personality, my personal skills, my relational skills. He called me into sales—selling life insurance.

I died a million deaths.

I remember making 90 cold calls a day. I was on commission, only commission, so I had no salary for almost ten years. I went to sleep scared. I woke up scared. I would shake at night, and Drenda would lay her hand on me. I thank God for Drenda, the greatest gift of my life. She believed in me, encouraged me, and greatly influenced my life, which kept me holding on and pressing forward. I knew I could not quit that job because God called me to it. I knew that He did.

Every day, I had to face myself. I was the issue, not the people I was talking to. I was the problem. I had a fear of man. I did not want to be rejected. I was not confident. So, I forced myself to make those calls. Eventually, I got better at it. I got better and better, and one day, our office became the number one sales office out of all 5,000 offices.

I did not know it had happened. I was not striving to be number one. There was no chart that said I was getting close to number one. They just called one day and said, "Guess what? You are the number one sales office out of our 5,000 offices; and we want you to speak at the national convention!" That was really amazing to me.

I had no idea what I would say in a speech. I did not know how I became number one. I was consistent every day with my numbers, and people could tell I was honest. But I figured they were anticipating a talk with some major principles or tactics, so I declined the opportunity.

Then, God called us to start a church. So now, I am dealing with even more people. I thought selling was tough until I started pastoring. Try going to bed sometime with 1000 people's problems on your mind instead of just your own. But Drenda and I learned how to give it to God and to pray for people, and we persevered.

But it was scary, to be honest. You pass one test in the Kingdom and then get a new assignment—twice as big. It is just like the Parable of the Talents. Once you learn how the Kingdom operates and you pass the test, you are given a new opportunity to put the same principles to work at a higher level with more territory.

It is always a challenge to face yourself and believe in God. You just have to put your trust in God to move forward. You cannot allow people's fears to entangle your life and what God has for you.

After we started a church, God called us to do television. For me, that was almost a deal-breaker. Television was the farthest thing from my mind. I still remember the first day we filmed. I was so intimidated that I could not sleep the night before we did our first program. It was tough. It was intimidating. But now, it has been something like 14 years of doing television, and it feels normal to me.

God has a great plan. Looking back on my life, I am amazed by all God has done through Drenda and me and by our simple "yes." And I believe He will amaze you with what He will do through your life too.

As you pass each test, God will keep giving you assignments. Which ones are you going to turn down? Which ones are you going to allow fear to stop you from embracing? Are you going to honor God and keep moving forward?

How you handle people qualifies you for the next assignment. You may be praying for promotion or increase, but that means you may have to change some things about how you deal with yourself, how you handle fear, and how you handle people.

I found that having employees was fun. But when you have employees, you have to train, mentor, and coach them. At times, you have to correct them. If you are insecure, like I was, you do not want to correct people because you want them to like you. But you cannot lead them unless you are willing to correct them. And God will never put you in a place where He cannot trust you with His prized possession—people.

God is in the people business, and you are in the people business. You may not realize it, but every business is a business to help people. If you want to start a business, find a way to help people. It is that simple. Find and solve a problem for people, and you have a business.

Life is about people, and there is nothing greater in life than people. The greatest thrills of life and your most significant memories will not come from anything you own but from your relationships with your family and friends and what you see God do in other people's lives.

I am not in any way trying to minimize the impact that people can negatively have on your life. They will hurt you. Satan will make sure that people mess with you. That is just how it is. But the Bible says that when you are persecuted, you should jump for joy, for great is your reward in heaven. People cannot stop you from succeeding. They cannot stop you from prospering. They cannot stop you from being healed. They cannot stop you from having a great marriage. They cannot stop you from any promise of God. They cannot stop you—unless you allow them to do so. Your family may abandon you or misread your motives, but God will never abandon you. Your friends may change, but God's Word never will.

When you make a decision that you are going to honor God with your life, you decide to push through the fear. Fear will try to entangle you and hold you back. So, you have to choose to go through it. It does not matter if you feel sick to your stomach. It does not matter if you are shaking in fear. You do not stop. You push through that fear.

Somewhere along the line, you have learned the vocabulary of fear. It is time to change that. You have to start telling yourself, "God is with me. I do not have to be afraid. With God, all things are possible to those who believe. I am a believer, so all things are possible for me."

I believe that God will never call you to something that He does not know you can handle. He will not take you past your ability. Of course, your ability does not mean your *personal* ability. It means the ability you and God have together. And I believe that as God calls you to different assignments, He will never call you to a place that He does not know you have the potential to capture.

You simply have to decide to get out of that bedroom and go down to the party. God is saying to you right now: "There is a party going on. There is a good life you can have if you will face your fear of people."

Yes, we have to deal with people. We have to learn how to work with people. When we honor God, He will honor us. He will make a way where it seems there is no way. You will have all you need, but it will involve the people He will bring to your side. We cannot let the fear of people interrupt our progress. So, make that decision now.

STEPPING BOLDLY INTO YOUR FUTURE

As we come to the end of this book, *Faith Over Fear*, I want to remind you of something crucial. The journey doesn't stop here. This isn't just the conclusion of a book. It's the beginning of a new chapter in your life. You've been equipped with the tools, the truths, and the strategies to overcome fear and step into the life God has designed for you. Now, it's time to put them into action.

Fear will try to reassert itself, whisper doubts, and stir up old anxieties. But you now know the truth—fear has no power over you. You've been given authority by God to trample on fear, to reject its lies, and to stand firm in the promises of His Word. You are not a victim; you are a victor. You are not defined by fear; you are defined by faith.

As you move forward, remember that living a life of faith is a daily choice. It's choosing to trust God even when the circumstances seem impossible. It's choosing to speak life over your situation, to declare God's promises, and to walk confidently in the destiny He has set before you. Every day is an opportunity to grow stronger in your faith and see fear diminish in the light of God's truth.

My prayer for you is that you will continue to grow in the knowledge of who God is and who you are in Him. I pray you will embrace the fullness of His love, power, and purpose for your life. And I pray that you will never settle for anything less than the abundant, fearless life that God has promised you.

The world needs what you have. It needs your story, your testimony, and your faith. So, go out there and make a difference. Be the light in the darkness, the voice of hope in a world filled with fear. You are God's chosen vessel; and with Him, there is nothing you cannot accomplish.

Thank you for joining me on this journey. Now, it's your turn to go out and live with faith over fear.

ABOUT THE AUTHOR

Gary Keesee is a television host, author, international speaker, financial expert, successful entrepreneur, and pastor who has made it his mission to help people win in life, especially in the areas of faith, family, and finances.

After years of living in poverty, Gary and his wife, Drenda, discovered the principles of the Kingdom of God, and their lives were drastically changed. Together, under the direction of the Holy Spirit, they created several successful businesses and paid off all of their debt. Now, they spend their time declaring the Good News of the Kingdom of God around the world through Faith Life Now, their organization that exists to motivate, educate, and inspire people from all walks of life and backgrounds to pursue success, walk out their God-designed purposes, and leave positive spiritual and moral legacies for their families.

Faith Life Now produces two television programs—*Fixing the Money Thing* and *Drenda*—as well as practical resources and conferences. Gary and Drenda speak at events around the world.

Gary is also the president and founder of Forward Financial Group and the founding pastor of Faith Life Church, which has campuses in New Albany and Powell, Ohio, and online.

Gary and Drenda, their five adult children and their spouses, and their grandchildren all reside in Central Ohio.

For additional resources by both Gary and Drenda, visit faithlifenow.com.

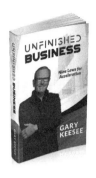

Get ready to discover how to accelerate your success and reach your dreams!

Did you know that over 80% of Americans don't like their jobs? So, why do they keep getting up each morning to go to a job that they hate? Because paying the bills has replaced their vision. Debt has hijacked their freedom and caused them to give up on their dreams.

Unfinished Business: Nine Laws for Acceleration puts everything on the table and walks you through the steps to change your mindset—your thinking—to one of opportunity and acceleration, so you don't leave any of your dreams, your impact, or your God-designed destiny unfinished.

With his combination of practical insights, stories, and Scriptures, Gary Keesee walks you through the simple steps to go from just surviving to thriving.

With over 30 years of experience, Gary has helped countless people realize their God-given dreams and purposes. He wants to help you win in life, take territory, and make sure that you leave no unfinished business behind.

Get your copy of *Unfinished Business* by going to faithlifenow.com.

Gary Keesee went from being completely desperate financially and very physically unwell to healthy and whole, paying cash for cars, building his home free from debt, starting multiple companies, and teaching hundreds of thousands of people about Kingdom living each week through television, ministry, and books just like this one.

What changed for Gary and how can it change YOUR LIFE?

Your answers are in the pages of THIS book series.

This isn't just another set of books with tips on how to fix your finances.

Full of fresh revelation, powerful examples from the Word of God, and inspiring personal stories about Gary and others who applied the foundational teachings from these five Kingdom principles in their own lives and experienced drastic change as a result, this series of books was written to help YOU experience real change in EVERY area of your life.

Join Gary Keesee on this incredible five-part journey of discovery that will completely revolutionize YOUR life... just like it did his.

This set contains paperback versions of Gary's complete Your Financial Revolution book series:
- *Your Financial Revolution: The Power of Allegiance*
- *Your Financial Revolution: The Power of Rest*
- *Your Financial Revolution: The Power of Strategy*
- *Your Financial Revolution: The Power of Provision*
- *Your Financial Revolution: The Power of Generosity*

Get your copy of the complete Your Financial Revolution five-book series at FaithLifeNow.com.

Get MENTORED for Success!
Join Team Revolution.

When you become a valued Team Revolution Partner, you help leave a lasting impact on lives all over the world while getting mentored for change in your own life!

You will hear from Gary Keesee, his wife, Drenda, and a team of experts and ministers in various fields to help you change and grow in faith, family, financial success, and business.

We believe you have a special destiny and calling, and joining Team Revolution puts you in a group of people who are committed to pursuing that destiny together.

As our partner, you are vital in helping us:

- **Provide Daily TV broadcasts that reach a potential of 780 million households worldwide.**

- **Produce life-changing resources that share Kingdom strategies for successful living.**

- **Support missionaries in third world countries, feeding the poor, supporting orphanages, working to stop sex trafficking in Eastern Europe, and so much more!**

LIVES CHANGED

"Our lives and church have been revolutionized through Gary and Drenda's teaching and mentorship! Our family is continually experiencing spiritual and financial breakthrough as we incorporate the Kingdom message they teach! Our church has experienced a 30% increase in our yearly receipts, we have purchased new acreage that doubles the size of our land, and we are about to break ground on a $6 million building project! We are so grateful for the impact Gary and Drenda have made in our lives!"

–Steve and Lisa

"The Lord spoke to me and said, "Daughter, you are blood of My blood. Bring your thinking into my Kingdom." I didn't understand what it meant at the time, but after listening to your teaching, you helped put the puzzle pieces together for me. You are teaching all about the Kingdom and God's way of doing things."

–Donna

"My life, marriage, family, and ministry experienced transformation when the spirit of poverty was broken, and Gary imparted a lifestyle of supernatural generosity to me."

–Leif

HOW DO I BECOME A PARTNER?

Becoming a ministry Partner is easy! Simply make your commitment via internet, phone, or mail.

- On the Internet, go to **www.FaithLifeNow.com** and click on the "Partnership" tab.

- By telephone, call us at **1.(888).391.LIFE.**

- By mail: **Faith Life Now, P.O. Box 779, New Albany, OH 43054**